The Journey Within

Srishti Agarwal

BookLeaf Publishing

India | USA | UK

ty to use, or
ency of the

ʒ Platform

Dedication

To those who struggle emotionally and need to love themselves a little more, and to those who believe in the power of belief itself— let's embrace the journey within.

Preface

"The Journey Within" is a collection of poems inspired by the emotions and stages we all may go through in our life. The poems are a reflection on the path towards self-discovery and throw light on how societal norms and pressures influence our being. As you find your way through the verses, you may be encouraged to look within and embrace every fragment that makes you who you are. With the hope to inspire, this collection is a celebration of our struggles and the strength they bring. Navigating these concepts through society, nature and emotions, it is a reminder to embrace the power we hold.

Acknowledgements

Heartfelt gratitude to all the people who have surrounded me with love and support through every stage of my life. My ongoing journey of self-discovery would be incomplete without you. Special thanks to all the readers for supporting this collection— it is the first time I am sharing my writing and it means the world to me if you have taken out the time to hold this book in front of you.

1. A Labyrinth

I am a labyrinth,
I am an illusion.

I am the saviour,
I am the solution.

Breaking free,
from the shackles within,
I find myself more
with every little win.

Where each victory
means one step less
to escape the labyrinth—
I am myself.

2. Look Within

Imagination is boundless;
the only boundary—
is you.

If you're stuck
in your old ways,
how can you ever
be new?

Lift your head,
but look within—
a world of magic
awaits to be seen.

3. Unaware

I see people running,
each to win a race—
unaware they're puppets
in society's embrace.

Running in sync, they think
the path is right.
To reach the destination first,
they'll put up a strong fight.

Uncontrollably out of breath,
they lose their way,
Forgetting who they were
and why they strayed.

The meaning of growth today
is skewed.
In pursuit of success, you forget
what makes you—you.

4. Wildfire

You are the sunlight
dancing on top of waves,
you are the whispers
the wind takes into caves.

Your smile is like a path
that runs a thousand miles,
spreading like wildfire,
kindling love—all bright.

Just like the ocean,
you go as far as you can see
If you think you're
bigger than the universe,
then that's what you'll be.

5. Chasing Sunsets

Like the sunsets I chase,
you're filled with colours of joy—
hues of pink, blue and yellow
painting your deep eyes.

Standing on a cliff,
I take in the light,
but I know as I turn,
you'll be out of sight.

The hues you leave
linger a little longer—
as if the sky stares at me,
with eyes— leaving me to ponder.

6. Leap Off

What is happiness
if you don't know yourself?

What is love
if you're afraid
to fall off the edge?

Knowing yourself
is the path less chosen.
Happiness is a culprit
overshadowing all emotions.

Take a leap,
see what shines.
Waiting to be unraveled
are emotions so divine.

7. A Spark

Between the black
and the white
lies a yellow—
a spark,
waiting to ignite.

Often consumed by darkness,
and faded by light,
society and its expectations
leave no respite.

It struggles to survive,
suppressed by the world
that claims to embrace its might.

But yellow is always
pressed underneath, so tight—
because the world knows
a spark can do much more
than just ignite.

8. A Sin Approved by God

All hail, in the temple of greatness—
a temple,
where wishes come true,
where the sins of few,
are forgiven,
where a lost soul finds direction,
where light overcomes dark,
like the first ray of dawn,
like he was to my soul.

There I was,
With him.

My only wish,
Is for his to come true.

But seconds later,
there's a pain in my chest—
clutching my heart
like the grip of a stabber

who stabs in the back.
My knees met the ground,
and suddenly I found
that my heart was put to rest.

I thought I was the light,
had no idea that I might
turn into —
A sin approved by god.

9. In Between

Hope,
lies in between.

In between
chaos and peace,
fears and dreams,
between who you are,
and who you want to be.

It begins after endings,
and leads you
towards beginnings.
It lies in between.

In between—
that's where I am.

Leaving the chaos,
moving towards peace,
overcoming my fears,

chasing my dreams.
Leaving who I was,
to become who I dream to be.

That's where I am,
with all the hope—
in between.

10. A Thousand Pieces

We're all like puzzles,
with a thousand pieces,

taking ages to be complete,
but the view? Worth it.

Then comes the wind,
throwing all pieces apart,

and impossible it seems
to find again, every part.

But where's the fun,
if the wind never blows
and there aren't dark nights?

How would you know
that in the dark, each piece
glows brighter than the sun's light?

11. Rebirth

I've climbed out
of that deep, dark well,
after falling so far,
flat on my back.

Neither could I see,
nor could I hear,
everything I was—
right before I disappeared.

I came back new,
yet wounded all over.
My hands worn out,
thoughts far from sober.

The lines defining my life
vanished like a dream.
With all the courage and pain,
I carved them back—
and felt like myself again.

12. Fragile?

A mirror is fragile,
until it shatters.

Falling to the ground
it's broken pieces
slit open the sky.

You look at yourself
from a place so far
overseeing the beauty
of fragments
that make you—
who you are.

13. Rise Again

I remember the darkness—
darker than the night
of a new moon's sky.
I remember the pain,
sharper than the knife
I almost used that day.

That day—
when I realised my worth;
when I understood
that if nothing else,
I could change myself.

My thoughts, my emotions,
my fears, my pain—
I knew it was time
to rise again.

To rise, to shine, to show
that no matter how deep I fall,

I can pick myself up again.
And no matter how long it takes to rise,
I am not afraid of falling again.

14. Unveil

The train passes by,
faster than time,
as I catch a reflection
on its window.

With eyes full of light,
a presence of charm—
she carried herself
like she owned the stars.

The train came to a halt,
and time stood still.
I looked into her eyes,
and realised—
they were my own.

What I longed for,
I always had.
Time just had to pause,
For me to unveil.

15. Moonlit dreams

The moonlight dances
with breezy winds.
Slipping through my window,
it enters my dreams.

Like a sliver of hope,
it lingers until morning.
When the sun's out
and my dreams
are still calling.

16. Belief

Belief is golden,
like that one ray
escaping a dark thundercloud.

Reflecting on water ripples,
it creates
an impact so loud.

It shines so bright,
bouncing
through every stone.

Nature truly has
a language
of its own.

17. Your Truth

Whether you think less of yourself
or more of others,

your truth is— yours to hold,
and with it you can do wonders.

The time has come,
to fix, to heal, to grow,

For you are the hero
in stories only you ought to know.

18. To be Lost

How sad is it
to be in a room full of people
and still feel alone?

To know you fit in,
yet still feel
like you don't belong.

To be everywhere
yet nowhere at all.

To be visible to others,
but invisible to yourself.

To be loved by everyone,
yet not enough
to make you feel
like you're worth loving.

Is this how it feels
to be lost?

19. Tug of War

The mind longs
to fly a thousand miles,
while the heart yearns
to chase priceless smiles.

The battle within
endures through life—
it's a tug of war
between happiness and pride.

The story is interesting—
for it's not a test
of milestones conquered,
but of the magic
you spread at your best.

20. The Cage Within

You fathom what it's like
to fly so high,
but scared of falling,
you don't embrace the sky.

Sometimes the cage,
is not outside
but within—
a barrier in your mind,
stopping the wind.

Just flutter a wing,
and see how you go
farther than the lands
of the curiosity you hold.

21. Lifetime

A lifetime—
is like a shooting star,
shining, fleeting, granting wishes,
Then vanishing, oh so far.

It passes through
in the blink of an eye,
with time just enough
to witness every sky.

But what about
the universe within?
Is a lifetime enough
to explore your own skin?